Legend of Loch Ness Monster for Kids

A Mystery in the United Kingdom

By Amber Richards

Table of Contents

Introduction

A fearsome creature lurks beneath the waters of the second largest loch (lake) in Scotland, at least that is the tale that has been re-told for hundreds of years. While most people are familiar with the pictures and stories from modern times, many do not realize these reports date all the way back to the 6th Century. That means for nearly 1500 years people have noticed something strange in and around the waters of Loch Ness. Scotland is part of the greater region known as the United Kingdom.

Loch Ness

Before we delve into the stories of the monster and resulting studies, it is important to understand a little more about the Loch itself. Loch Ness is located in the Scottish Highlands, an area well known for legend and mystery, the Loch is the largest body of fresh water in Britain. The loch itself spans over 23 miles and contains roughly 16 million 430 thousand gallons of water! To reach the bottom of Loch Ness you would need to be able to dive 754 feet, which is possible to dive with the proper equipment and training, but leaves a diver in a dark murky world, where their field of vision is limited to the scope of their underwater lights and torches.

Other facts about Loch Ness:

Tectonic Lake resulting from shifting plates in the earth's crust 14,000 acres – surface area Loch Ness could contain ten times the current world population. Due to depth and volume of water the Loch never freezes. Winter time at Loch Ness can be a bit eerie as the lake appears to steam

Hills surrounding the Loch still rise by 1mm per year.

Urquhart Castle

Along the northern shore of Loch Ness lies the

ruins of Urquhart Castle, built sometime between

the 13th and 17th century. While this is much

later than some of the earliest references to the

Loch Ness monster legend, there is some scientific evidence that an earlier fort sat on the outcropping and housed an early Pict King, Brude the Brave and True. This is where the history of the castle and the Loch Ness Monster first cross paths.

Encounters with Loch Ness Monster

St. Columba was a holy man from Ireland who traveled to the land of the Picts in the Scottish Highlands on many occasions. Tradition states that St. Columba was involved in a disagreement with St. Finnian over the right to keep a psalter (book of Psalms) he had copied from an original under Finnian. In the course of the dispute, a battle was fought in which many lives were lost. After the battle of Battle of Cúl Dreimhne there were many who wanted St. Columba tossed out of the church, instead he was allowed to dedicate his life to sharing the gospel as a missionary in an attempt to convert as many

men as lost their lives in battle.

St. Columba exiled himself to Scotland and

during one of his many trips down the Loch he

observed some locals burying a man they insist

was killed by a hideous beast from the depths

and another swimmer was currently in danger

from the monster. At this report St. Columba

waded into the deep and stopped the Loch Ness

monster with the sign of the cross and a

command: "Thou shalt go no further, nor touch

the man; go back with all speed" Men along the

banks swore the beast instantly stopped and

retreated to the depths as if pulled by massive

ropes!

Modern Sightings

Of course, in the days of St Columba there was

no such thing as a camera of any kind, which

means the truth of the claims will never be able

to be verified. Thankfully, people are still curious

about the mystery surrounding the loch and over the years, there have been a couple of sightings that include photographic "evidence".

1933: Hugh Gray was taking a stroll beside the loch when he noticed some serious splashing in the water. He quickly grabbed his camera and took several pictures of the commotion. Unfortunately, only one of the images came out and experts have been unable to agree on whether it is a dog swimming for shore or a large eel like creature.

1934: If you have ever seen a photograph of the Loch Ness Monster, this is probably the one. Dubbed the Surgeons Photograph it was supposedly taken by a London physician and shows a grainy image of the head and neck of the Loch Ness Monster. Many different theories have been presented about what is truly in the image, most claiming it is a hoax, which was proven true when one of the co-conspirators made a deathbed confession about how the "monster" was created.

1938: An African tourist captured three minutes of 16mm film depicting what he claimed was the monster. Though he refused to show the images to investigators, he did eventually publish a single image in his book and a noted biologist claimed it was positive proof.

What did these people capture on film? Have they truly encountered the creature from the deep? One might wonder why the creature spoke of in the 6th century was ferocious, dragging people beneath the waters in full view of everyone but today the monster is elusive and secretive. Is the same Loch Ness monster still lurking around the deep dark waters of the Scottish Loch or are the current sightings offspring who have learned to be more cautious? These questions and many more are what stir people from around the world to seek out the truth behind the loch ness monster!

Myths, Legends and Stories

You may be wondering why Scotland or why this particular body of water. After all, why couldn't there be a Lake Erie Monster or Mississippi River Creature? Part of the reason may be the fact that this part of the world is steeped in myths, legends and lore. For hundreds of years stories of mystical creatures both big and small have been passed down from generation to generation. In the area of Loch Ness alone there are many stories of fairy Queens, healing pools, Kelpies, water sprites and much more.

Fairy Queen Caoihme

One myth that some people consider is that of fairies. The legend goes like this: fairies who long to reach out and communicate with their human counterparts, but most of the time their presence is met with fear, ridicule or harassment. Over the years, the fairy folk have become much more selective when choosing a messenger to carry their profound knowledge to the human race. In fact, centuries often pass with no contact between the two worlds.

Centuries had passed with no contact, as the

fairies searched for a human worthy of the task.

Many of the fairies recalled a gentle healer,

known as Bebhinn. Her reputation as a healer

and gentle soul prompted the Fairy Queen

Caoihme to contact Bebhinn through her dreams.

The latter would be tasked with coming to the

land of the fairies through her dreams and carrying the knowledge back to her fellow man. The queen requested Bebhinn to journey north to the great loch. Once she arrived, she made camp on a well-known rocky outcrop and there she entered the world of the fairy.

Fact and Fiction?

Was this the same rocky outcropping that would later be the sight of Urquhart castle? Was fairy magic afoot in and around the famous loch that soon boasted a beast of unknown proportions? The legend goes that Bebhinn shared the stories, knowledge and healing she learned from the fairy queen up until the day she died, when she was transported to the land of fairies and her ancestors.

Kelpies

Could the loch ness monster actually be a large water horse? In Scottish legend and myth, there are stories of kelpies. Descriptions vary but generally, the kelpie appears as a lost horse, black, white or green in color with hide as smooth as a seal and constantly dripping water. These creatures sole goal is to lure people into the depths of the water, and they are particularly fond of children!

Kelpies are said to be able to transform

themselves into beautiful women in order to lure

men to the depths and they also have the unique

ability to create illusions in order to remain

hidden from the naked eye.

However, there have been no modern references

to people losing their life to the Loch Ness

monster, could these two legends be one in the same? It would explain the random sightings, if Nessie (as sometimes the Loch Ness monster is called) has the ability to create illusions and hide from people the chances of spotting the elusive creature would be slim indeed.

Scientific Studies

In 1987, the largest sonar exploration of any freshwater body in the world began. Operation Deepscan was a cooperative effort between Adrian Shine, leader of the loch ness project and Darrell Laurence, head of Laurence Electronics based in Tulsa Oklahoma. The plan was to use Laurence's sonar technology to scan the depths of Loch Ness from one end to the other, in hopes of finding the monster from the deep.

Twenty-four boats would take part in this exploration, all equipped with Laurence's X-16 sonar equipment that would record everything on paper for further analysis. The range of this equipment was 1300 feet, more than enough to probe the depths of the loch.

Results:

Three strong contacts were made on day one

Range of depth was 256 ft. to 590 ft.

Best contact was made opposite of Urquhart Bay

Size of contacts was larger than any reported species living in the loch.

Day 2 resulted in no contacts, which is important because it means whatever they found on day one had moved and was not semi-stationary.

Some say Operation Deepscan was a bust; after all, they were unable to produce the Loch Ness Monster for the entire world to see! However, there is just enough evidence to keep skeptics guessing and true believers hoping for the next sighting of the legendary creature.

BBC 2003

In 2003, the BBC decided to settle once and for all the debate about the Loch Ness Monster Legend. Using sophisticated sonar and satellite technology researches swept the entire loch, from end to end and side to side. Over 600 separate sonar beams were used in the search for Nessie, to no avail. They discovered the loch is steeply sided with a flat bottom, but nothing more.

Hunt for Hidden Animals

What are some reasons these scans of the loch are returning such dismal reports? Loren Coleman, believes he has some possible and plausible answers. Coleman is a world known crypto zoologist, which is just a fancy way of saying he is someone who studies hidden animals. Here are a few of his ideas about the loch ness monster:

The creature or creatures do not live in the lake full time, it is a narrow lake and full time residence is unlikely.

The ocean is approximately a mile from the loch, the animals could live in the ocean and come to the loch intermittently.

There have been land sightings of the beast. Coleman believes the Loch Ness Monster could actually be a very rare long necked seal.

What We Know

No one has conclusively proven the existence of the Loch Ness Monster, leaving many to believe it is mere legend at best or a marketing ploy at worst. While it is true that the monster has drawn many people to the banks of the Loch, it is hard to imagine that a 6th Century missionary could have had that much foresight! So what do we know about Nessie?

Since earliest times there have been approximately 4000 reports of sightings. The first recorded reference is from the 6th century, meaning any modern monster is likely offspring and not the original. New animal species are being discovered every day, beaked whales, large sea cows and much more. Loch Ness is deep enough to hide a creature of considerable size.

Alastair Boyd discovered the Surgeons Photo was a hoax, but due to his own sighting remains and avid believer in the Loch Ness Monster. He asserts that what he saw was an animal at least 20 ft. in length.

The Search for the Loch Ness Monster will continue!

What Do You Think?

Is Nessie a pre-historic animal who was trapped in the Loch for hundreds, or thousands of years? Could this creature be a fabled beast like an oversized Kelpie or some other being we have yet to hear about? To wrap up this journey to the deep waters of Loch Ness, here are a few common myths surrounding the monster:

Trapped since dinosaurs - during the last ice age Scotland was covered by tons of ice, very unlikely that a dinosaur could have survived in the loch under the ice for thousands of years.

Solitary- Nessie is not likely a solitary animal, for starters the first sightings were centuries ago and if we know anything about animals it is that they need others of their own kind to survive.

Plesiosaurus- There is a popular theory stating the Loch Ness Monster is actually a plesiosaurus, but these are air-breathing creatures, which would mean very frequent trips to the top.

Create Your Own Myth

Perhaps the greatest thing about the Loch Ness Monster legend is the fact that you can actually create your own story surrounding the beast if you like. What do you think the truth is behind the creature?

I like to think that perhaps he or she is a beloved mascot for the Scottish Highlands and the reason the sightings are so rare is because the locals are protecting the animal. Have they built a series of underground tunnels for Nessie?

Many people don't realize this, but there are other parts of the world that have legends and folklore of loch ness type monster sightings as well. The Loch Ness in Scotland is the most famous however.

Some of the others are:

Mokele – Mbembe, Africa

Ogopogo – Lake Okanogan, British Columbia

Canada

Monster Issie or Ishii – Lake Ikeda, Japan

Champ or Champy – Lake Champlain, Burlington

Vermont USA

Lake Monster – Lake Van in Eastern Turkey

Lake Chonji Monster – Lake Tianchi – North

Korea

So there are more to research if you'd like to.

Whatever, you think about the loch ness

monster and all the sightings, one thing is

certain, it is a great story to spark your imagination!

The End

If you enjoyed this book or received value from it in any way, would you be kind enough to leave a review for this book on Amazon? I would be so grateful. Thank you!

89351990R00024

Made in the USA
Lexington, KY
27 May 2018